ABC MONS[...]!!

THE A IS FOR AAAAAAHH!!!

THE Z IS FOR Zither...

BY MR. REESE

For:

Heather, Isaac,

JJ, Karl,

Levi, Mea,

Nathaneal, Paul,

and Zoe,

The Real ABC MONSTERS.

Swiftly Sneaking,
Tiny or Tall,
Lots are Lurking,
Down the Hall...

Smooth and Bumpy,
Jagged or Round,
They Fly through the Air,
They Crawl on the Ground...

Try to Find Them.
Open the Door.
They'll let you Know,
What the Alphabet's for!

26 Monsters,
Are Plain to See!
Can you Spot them All,
From A to Z?

THE **A** IS FOR...

AAAAAAHH!!!

IT'S AN

ALIEN ATTACK!!!

I CAME DOWN HERE FROM

A FAR OFF STAR

AND YOU CAN'T SEND ME BACK!!!

AAAAAAHH!!!

What's the Buzz
about the BEEVi?
What's the Buzz
coming from the Bees?
What's the Buzz
about the BEEVi?
He's got such
Big Blue Eyes!
We all agree.

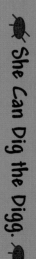

THE **DiGG** DIGS IN THE DIRT.

THE **DiGG** EATS LOTS OF BUGS.

THE **DiGG** JUST CAN'T BE HURT,

BECAUSE HE'S OH, SO SMUG.

THE **DiGG** IS REALLY SMART,

'CAUSE HE NEVER DOES NO DRUGS!

CAN YOU COUNT ALL THE HOLES

THAT THE **DiGG** HAS DUG,

AND CAN YOU COUNT ALL THE

BUGS THAT BUG THE **DiGG**?

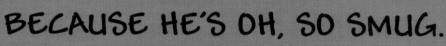
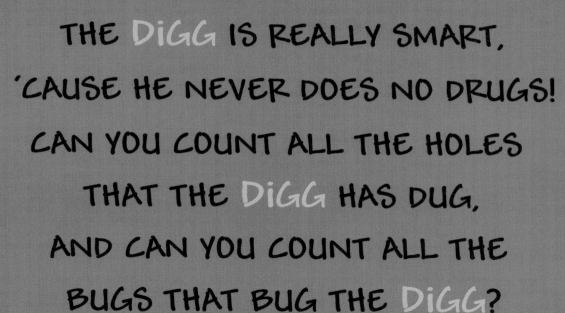
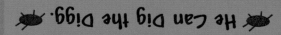

BONK! CRASH! BIFF! OOF! SMASH! BANG!

THE **Feela** IS FAIRLY UNIQUE.

BONK!

HE FREQUENTLY WALKS IN HIS SLEEP!

SNORE...

HE CAN GIVE YOU QUITE A FRIGHT,

EEK!

'CAUSE HE SOMETIMES GOES BUMP

IN THE NIGHT!

OUCH!

ZONK! POW! OUCH! BOFF! SMACK! STOMP!

OW! CLANG! CRUNCH! BREAK! SQUISH!

WONK! RIP! TEAR! STUB! SLAM! CRACK!

 Oh, Gee! Look at the

Gigant!

He's bigger than a Whale.

He sits and sits and sits aaaaaall day,

On his Ginormous tail.

They'll give you the
HEEBIES.
They'll give you the
JEEBIES.
They'll give you the
CREEPIES,
and keep you from your
SLEEPIES!

HEEBIE JEEBIES

What is IT!?

What is IT!?

I'd really like to know!

What is IT!?

What is IT!?

Will it bite me on the toe?

IT!

That Jibberin' Jabberin' Jub Jub!

He soaks all night in the Tub Tub!

He eats up all the Grub Grub!

And he gives his tummy a Rub Rub!

'Cause he's the

Jibberin' Jabberin'

Jub Jub!

Jub Jub

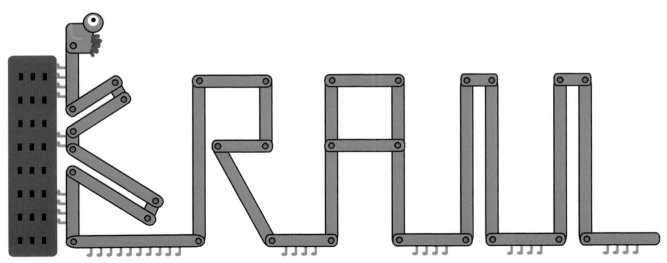

The Lickarish

likes to lick candies,

with it's long,  long sticky tongue.

It licks up all the lovely sweets,

the lemon drops, and gum!

The Mea is a monster!

Who's pretty as can be.

She wears a purple tutu,

and has great big sharp teeth!

Oh, have you seen the

Ooh Lah Lah?

She can be very shy,
But if she tries to hide from you,

Just look for a Big Pink Eye!

Try to spy the Ooh Lah Lah,

And she'll fly into the sky!
She'll zip away so fast today,

That you won't see Eye to Eye!

The
PAW PAW

has 2 **paws,**

and each paw has 3 **claws,**

and each claw has 3 **hairs,**

and each hair is on its **pair**

of **Purple Paws.**

PAW PAW

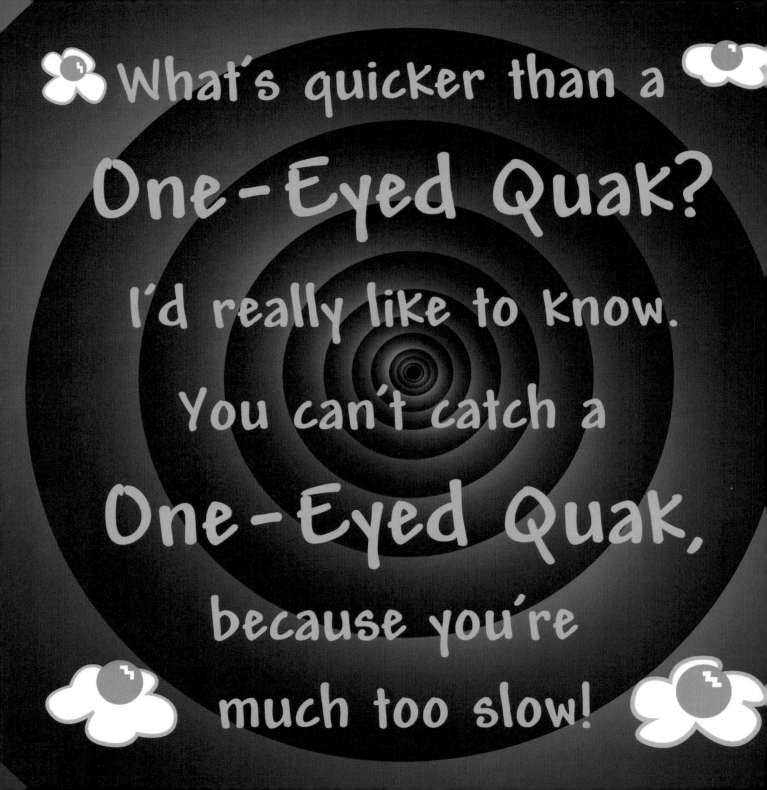

If you run across the
Rad Red Ravennus,
Who rules the
Red Haired Radishes,
Who wriggle in the ground,
Then you'd really better run away
Whenever they're around!

RAVENNUS

The Triclod
has 3 toes.
The Triclod
has no nose.
He stomps across the countryside,
And smashes houses
with 3 sides!

ndergator

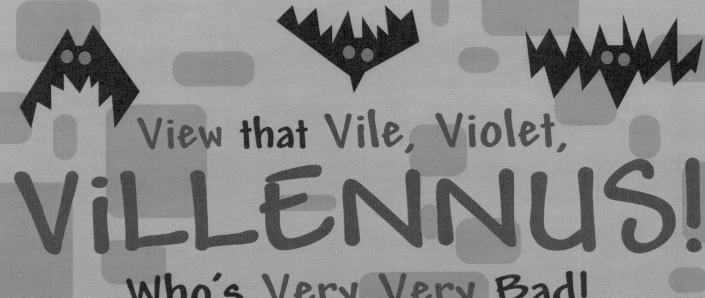

View that Vile, Violet,

ViLLENNUS!

Who's Very Very Bad!

He comes from Transylvania!

His Daddy's name is Vlad!

He's like a Vicious Vampire!

Who Vants to suck your Blood!

Don't stand around all Vulnerable!

 Go hide down in the Mud!

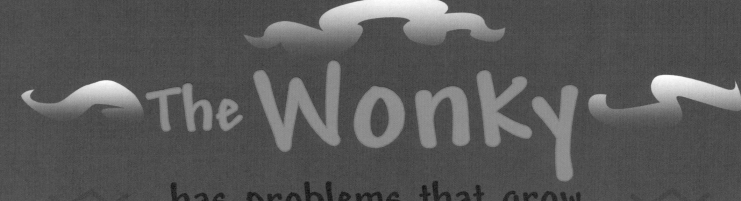

The Wonky

has problems that grow.

It doesn't know which way to go!

One head likes to go with the flow.

The other goes where the wind blows.

While one head goes to,
and the other goes fro,

its middle don't know where to go!

IN THAT BOX THERE IS A

XOX!*

HE'S THE ONE WHO ATE YOUR

SOCKS!

THAT XOX WAS SMARTER THAN A

FOX,

TO HIDE INSIDE A TINY

BOX!

"XOX" SOUNDS LIKE "ZOCKS"

Why don't you know that

Yellow Monster?

- It **Yips** just like a dog.

- It **Yaps** just like a cat.

And it **Yops** just like a frog!

It **Yodels** and it **Yammers,**

And **Yorts** just like a hog.

- It **Yells** and **Yipes** and **Gripes** at **You,**
And

Yips and Yaps and Yops!

¡IP! ¡AP! ¡OP!

.....the Zither...............

....goes hither and thither

......it slithers in all kinds of weather.........................

.....it goes over there...

..............................and it slides thru your hair.

.....it goes over yonder..

....wherever you wander

.....and whether you'd rather..

....it leave you alone.

......it slithers right into your home.............................

The ABC MONSTERS
have come here to play,
but now it is time
to call it a day.
It was kind of scary,
but also was fun,
and now
all the letters are done!

THE END.

Email: ALPHABETMONSTERS@GMAIL.COM

Check for MR. REESE BOOKS on AMAZON.COM

Made in the USA
San Bernardino, CA
18 October 2013